To Max –
of course.
—

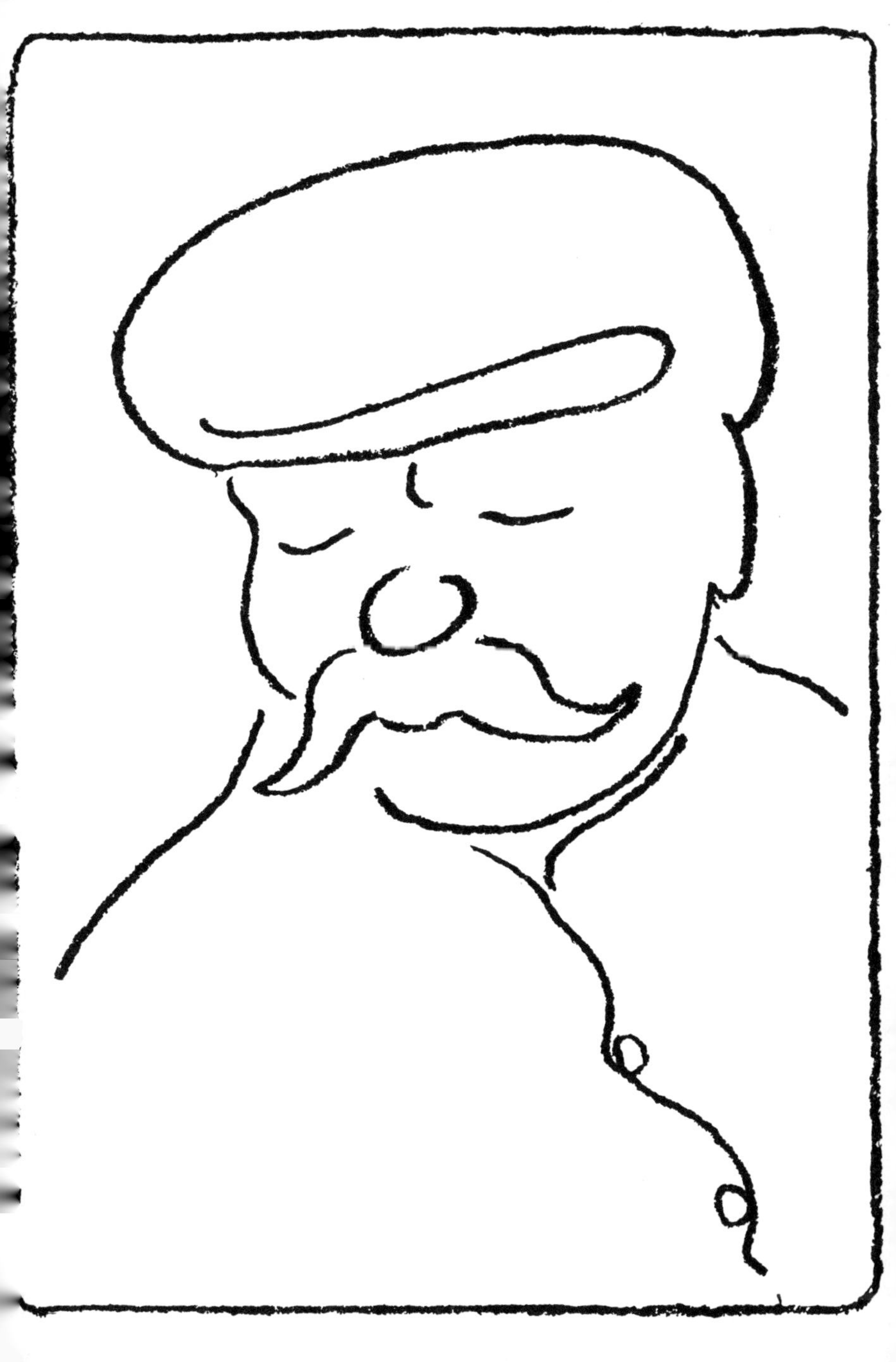

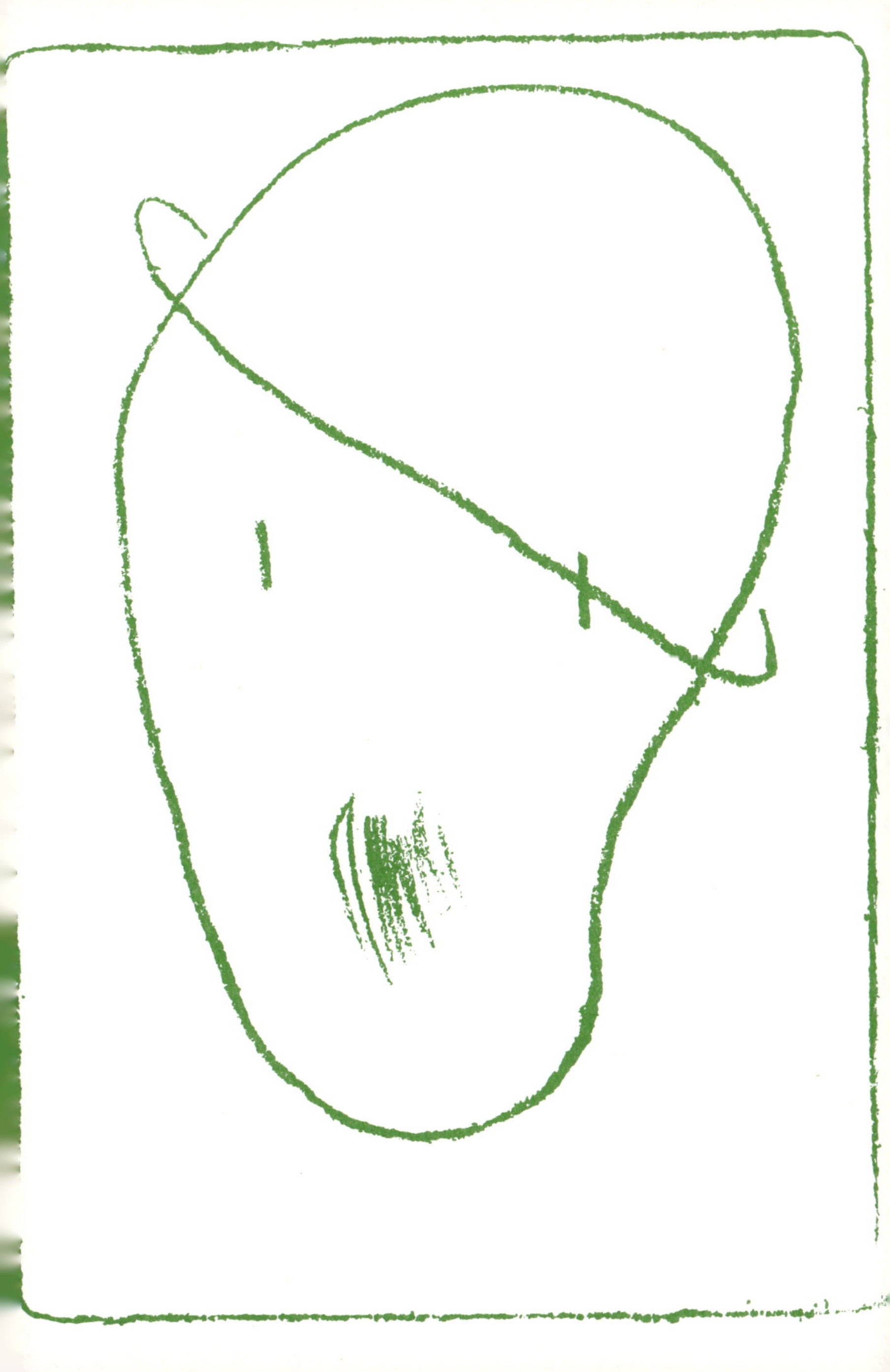

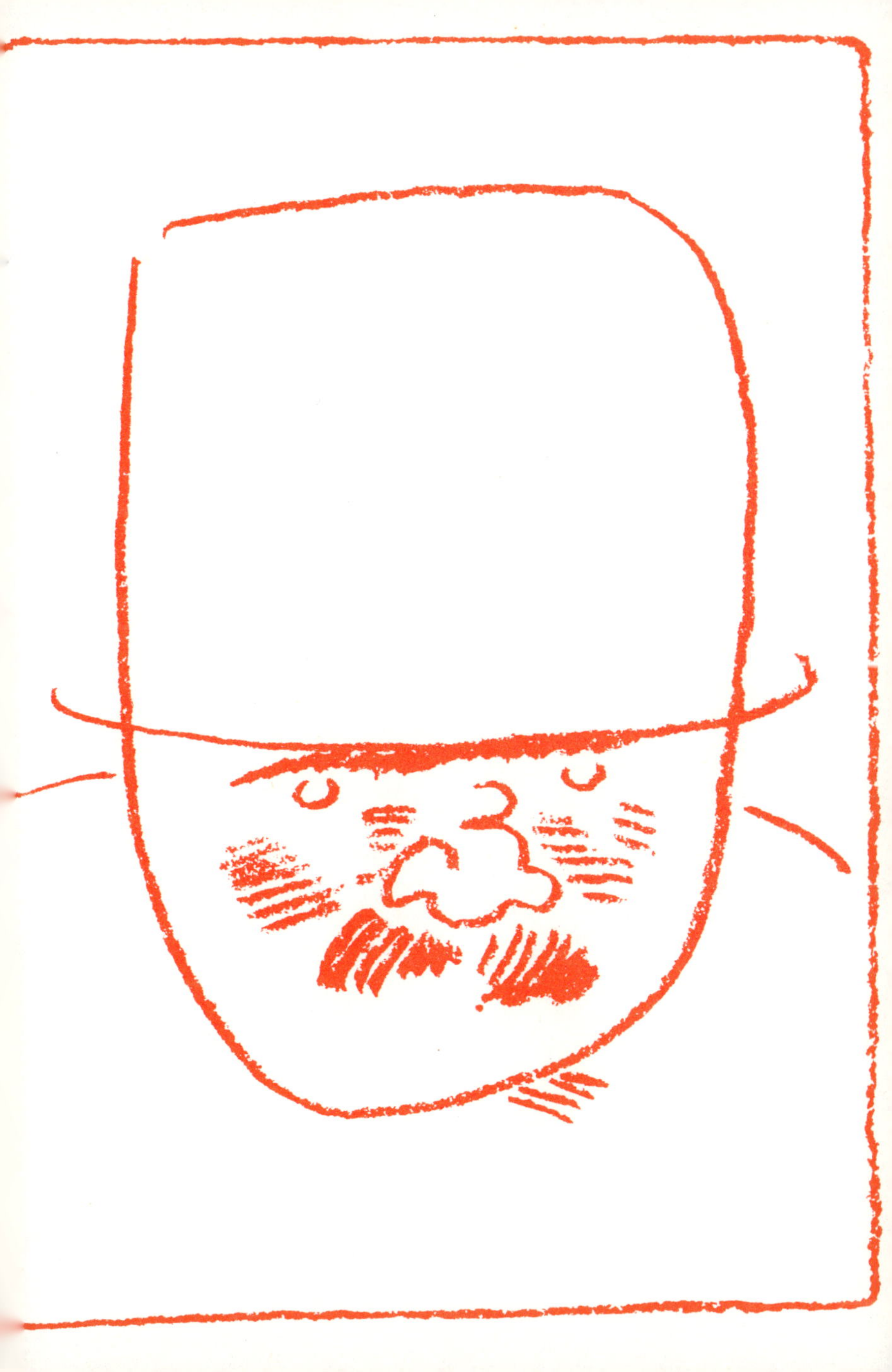

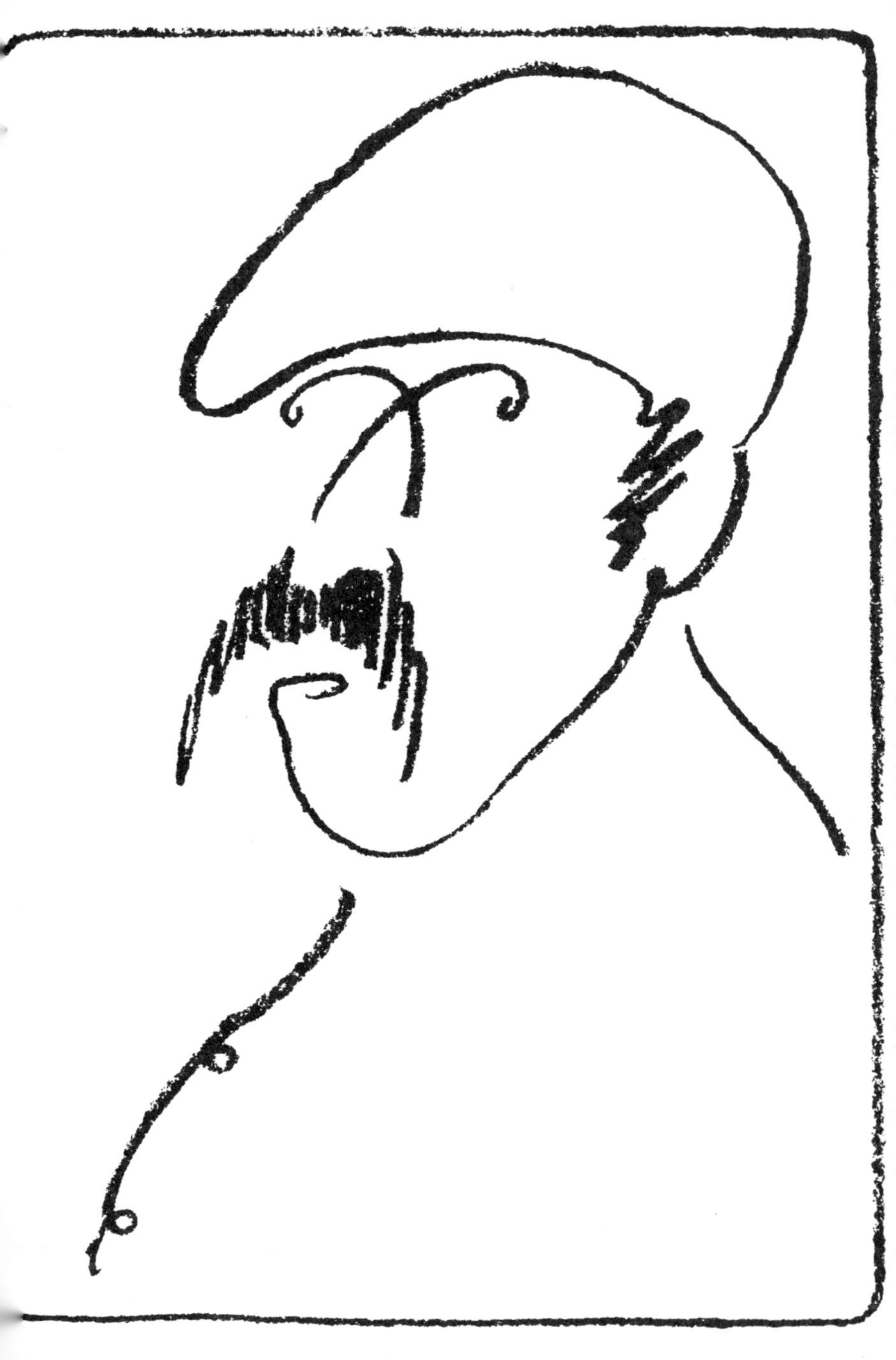

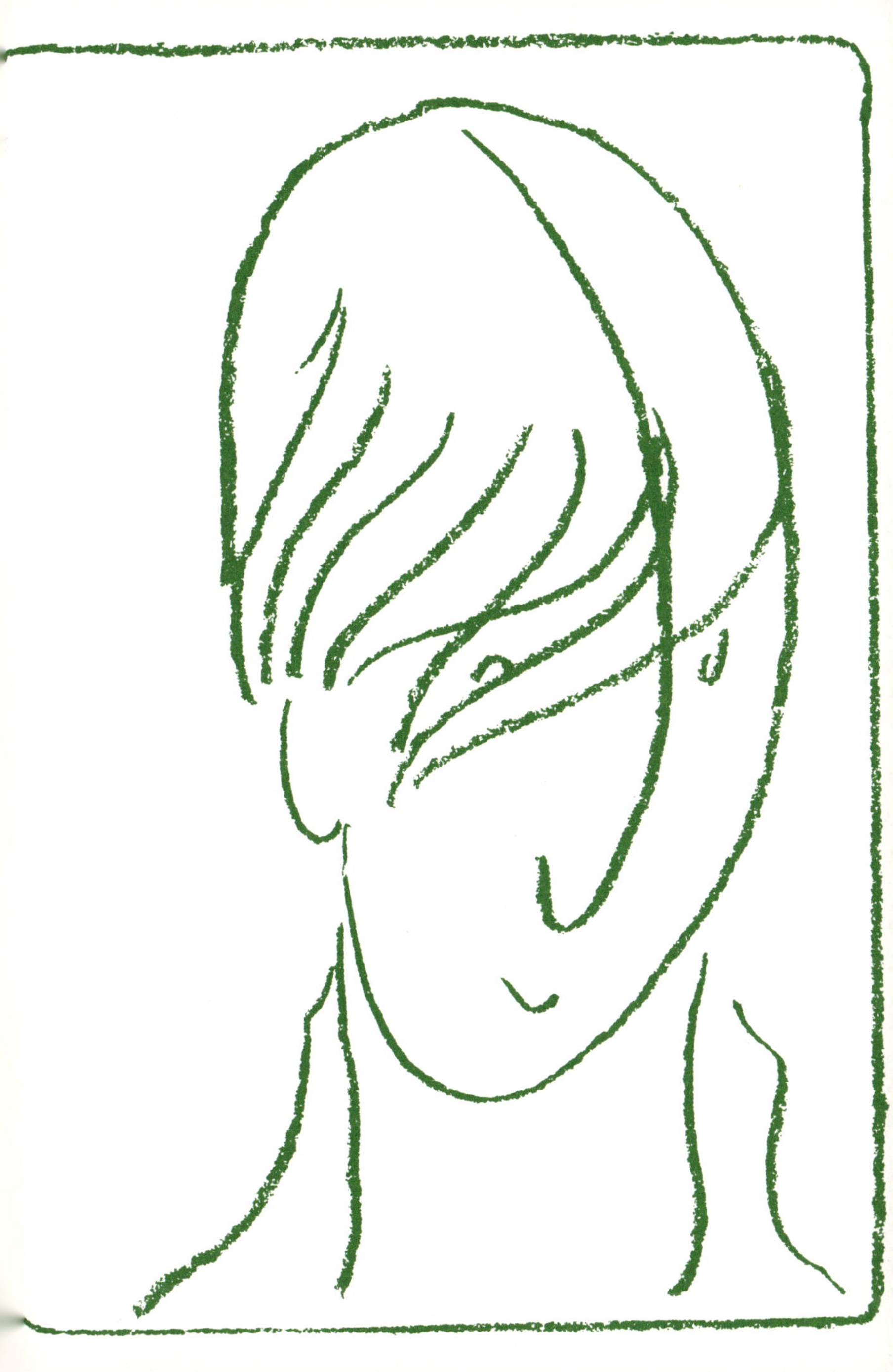

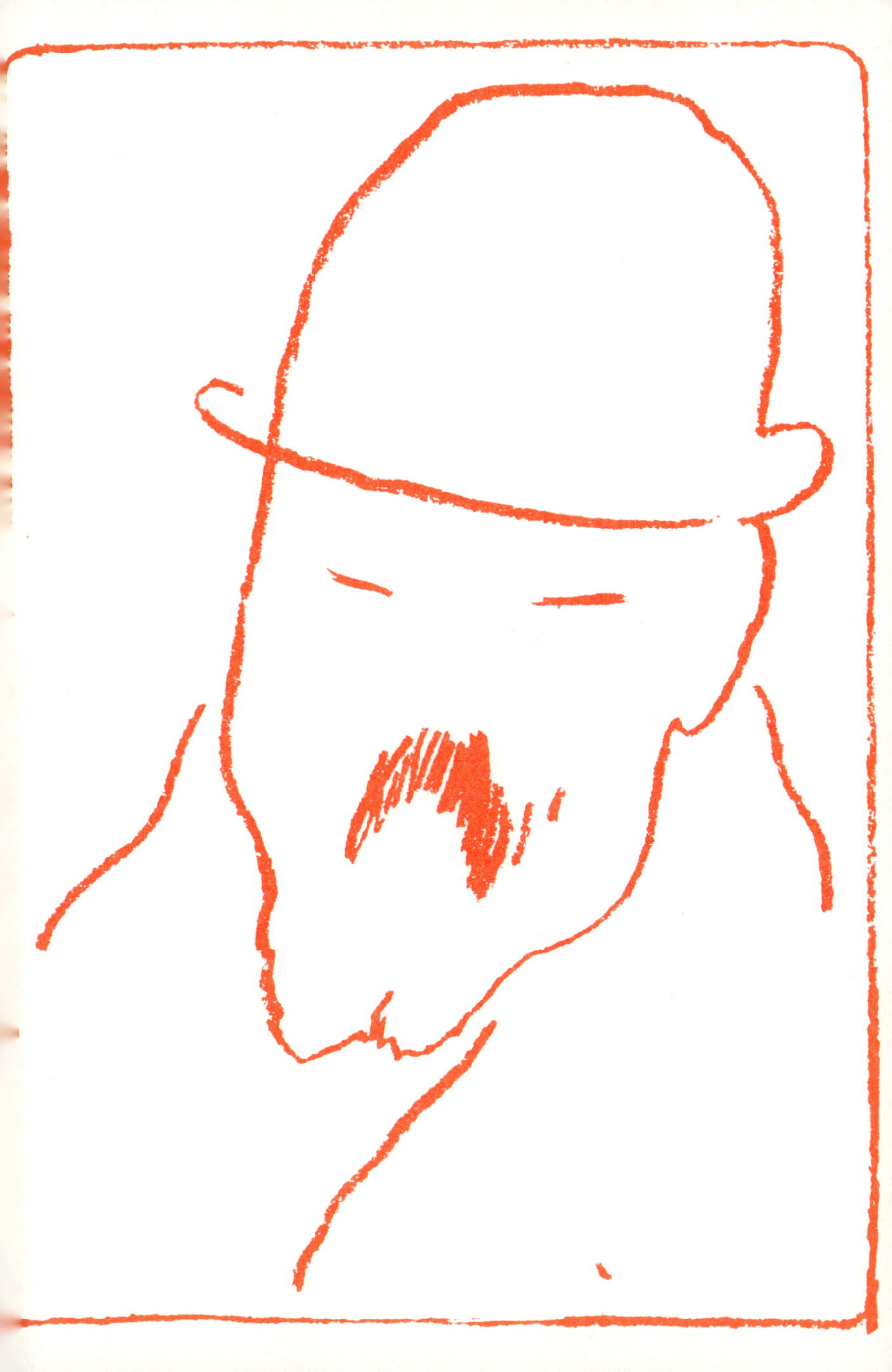

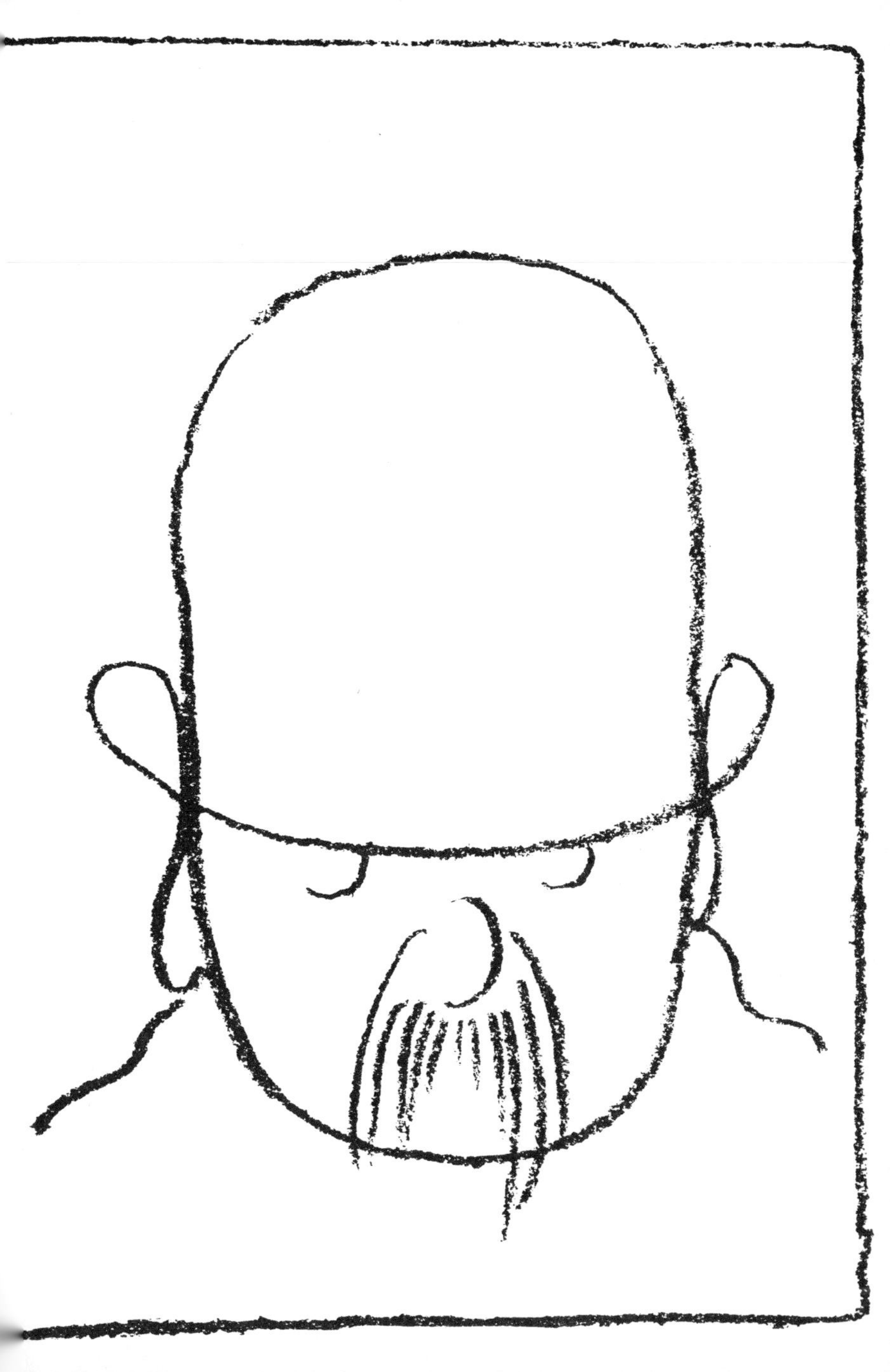

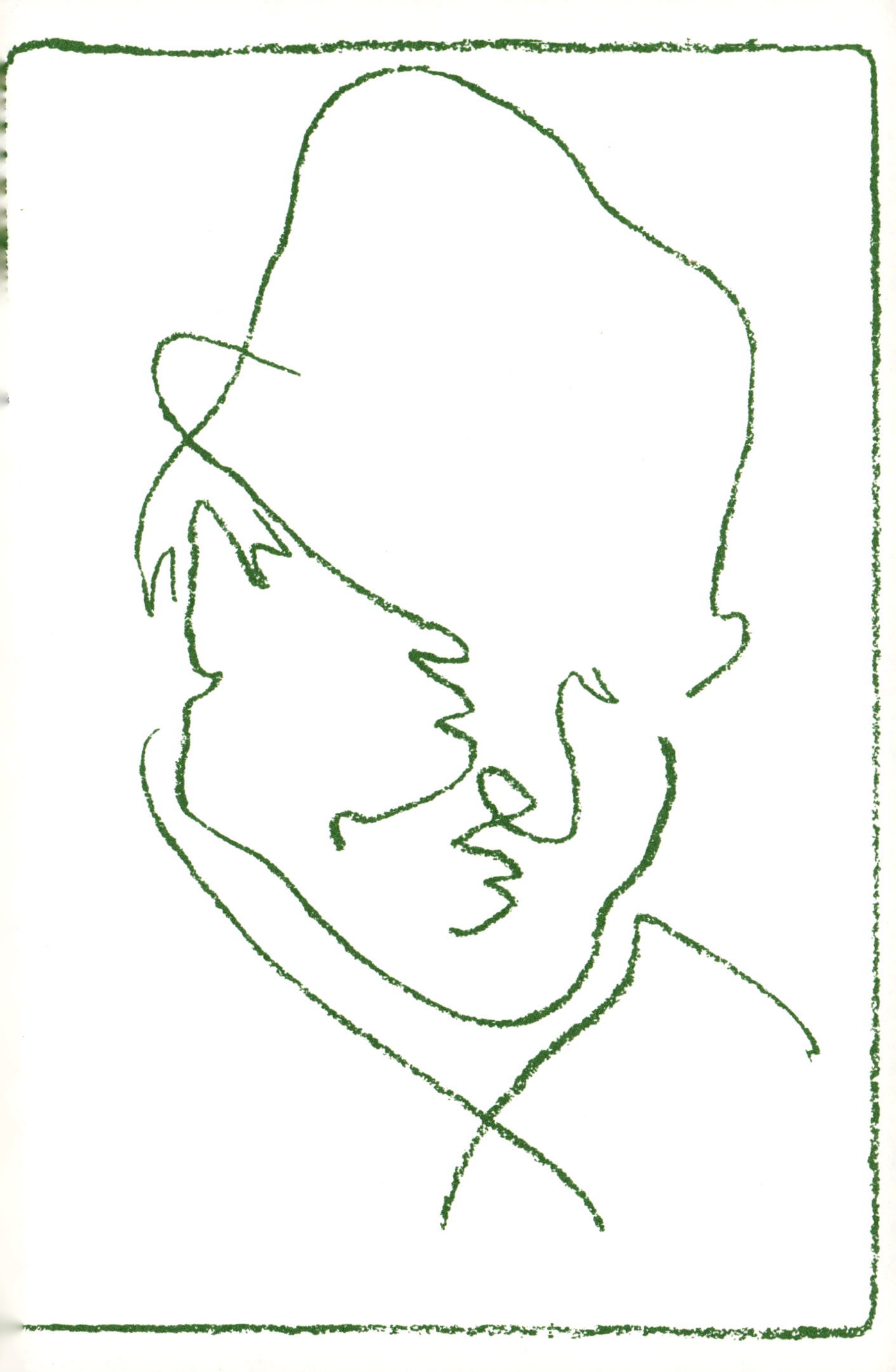

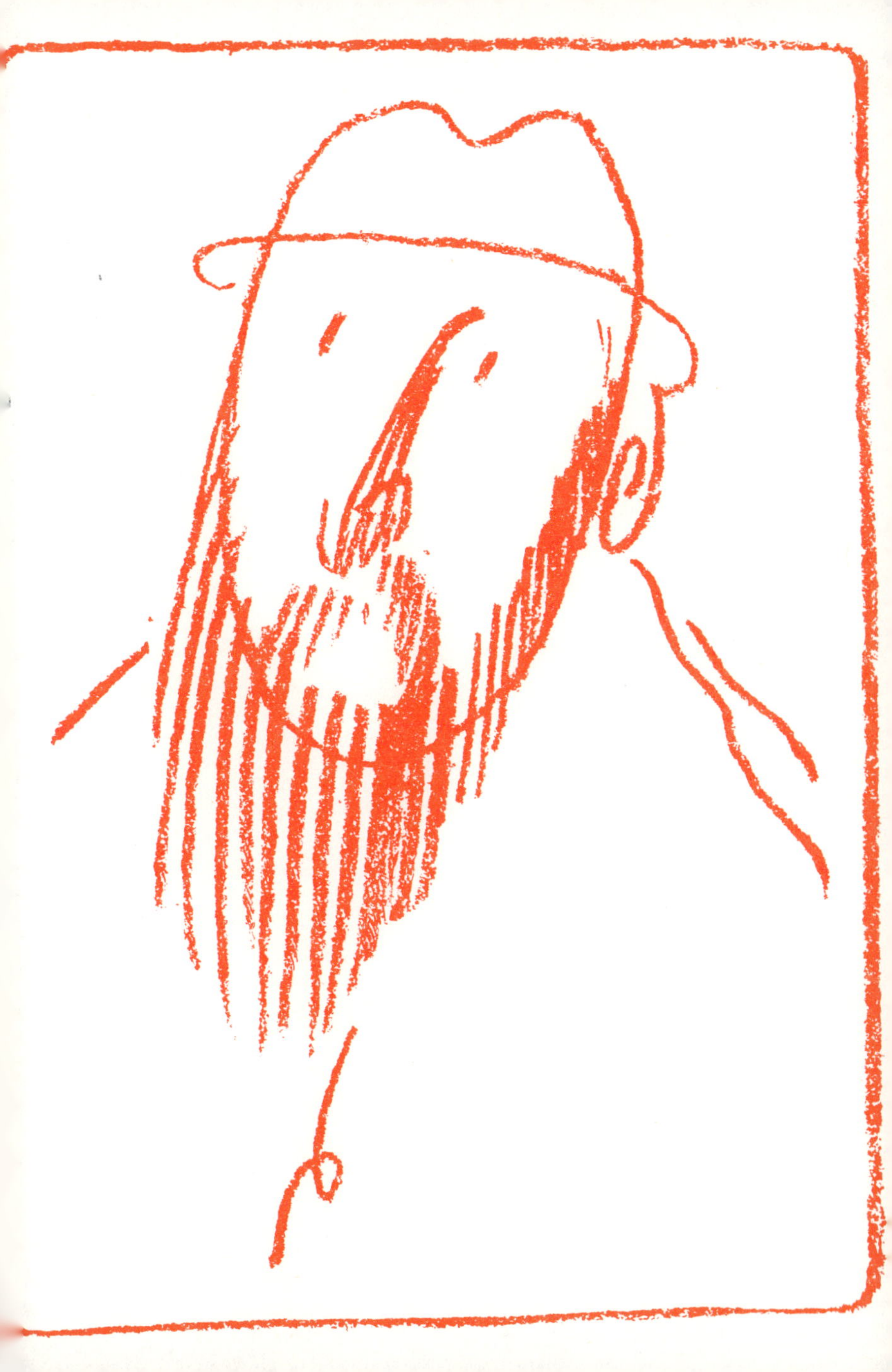

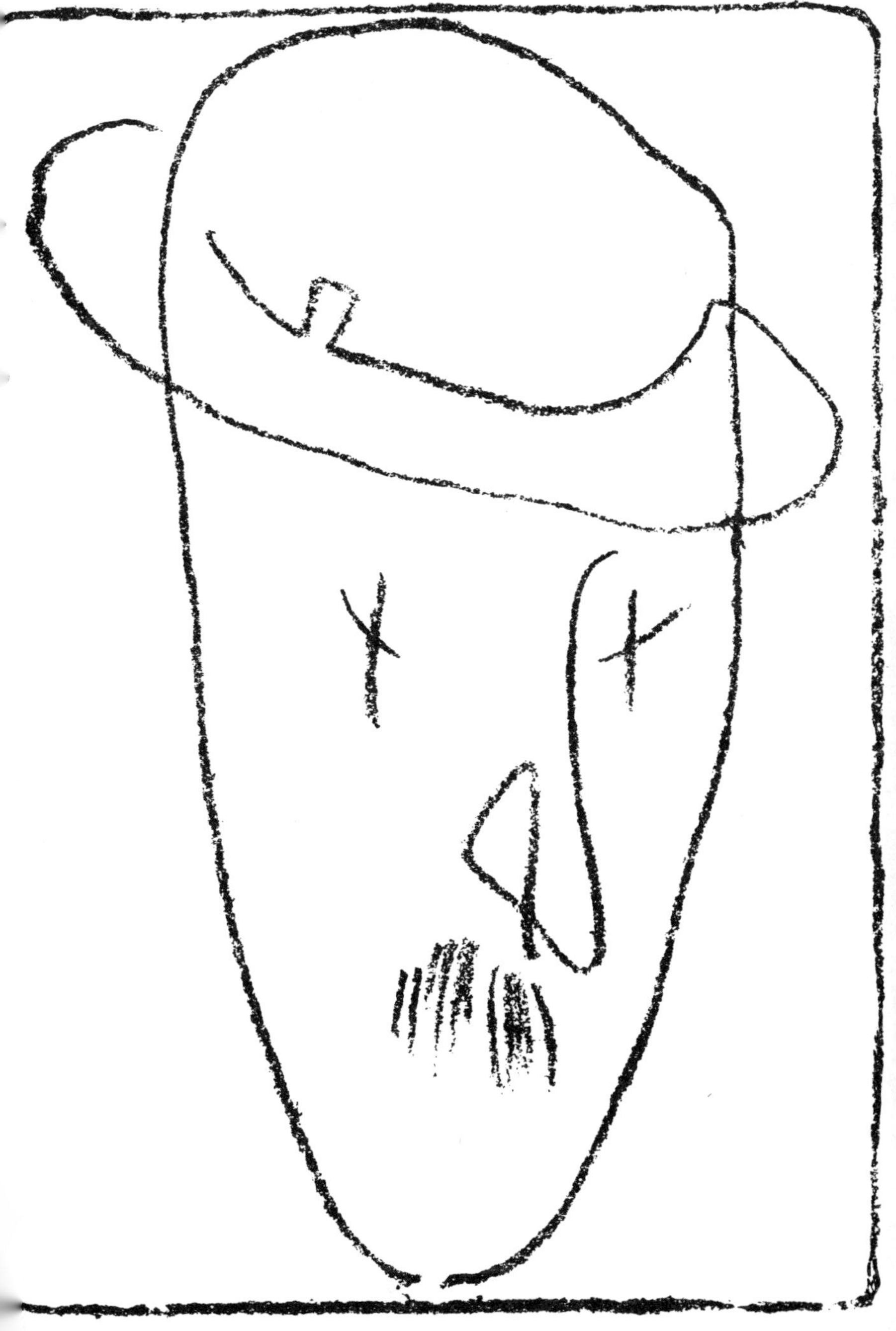

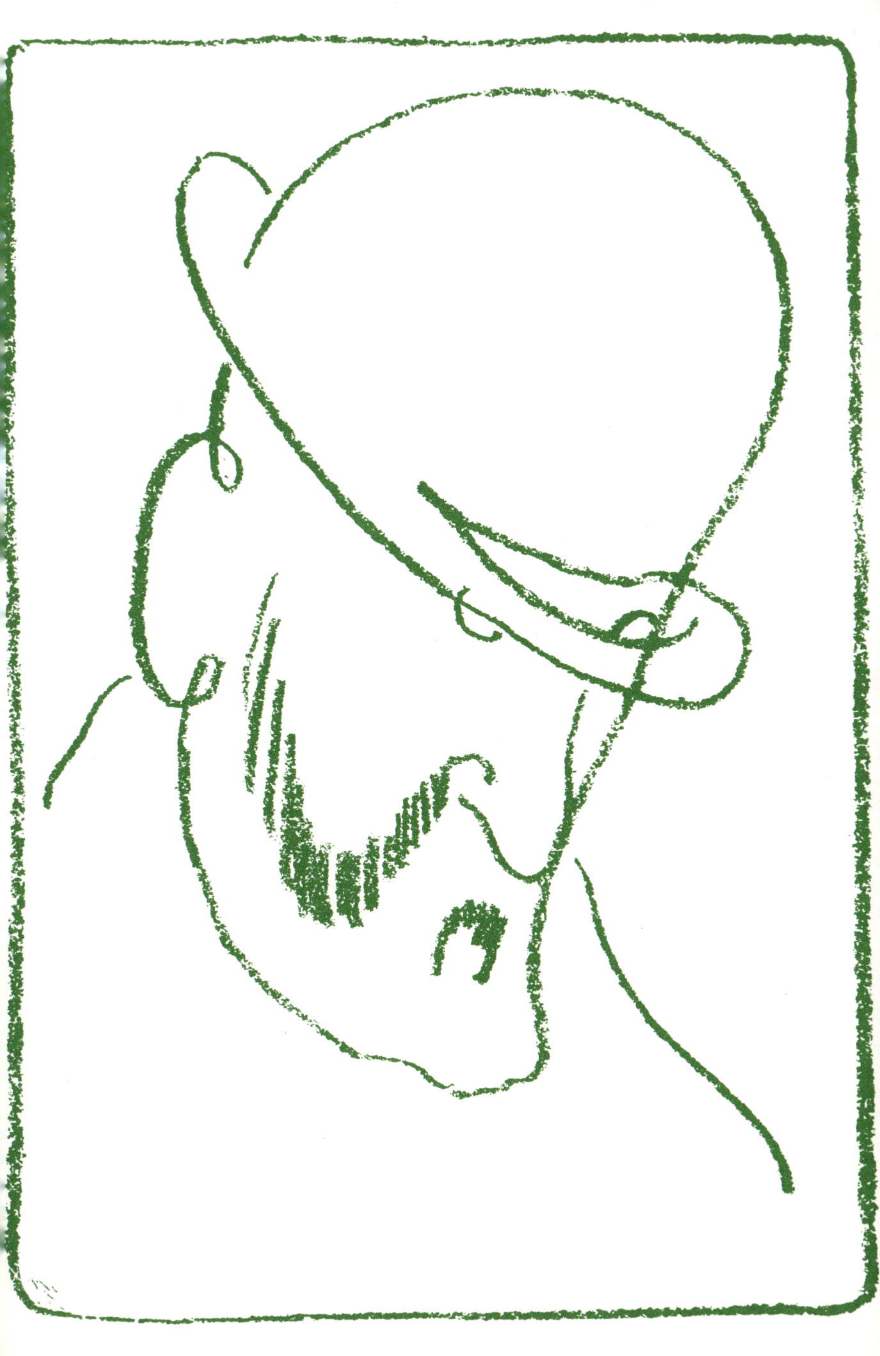

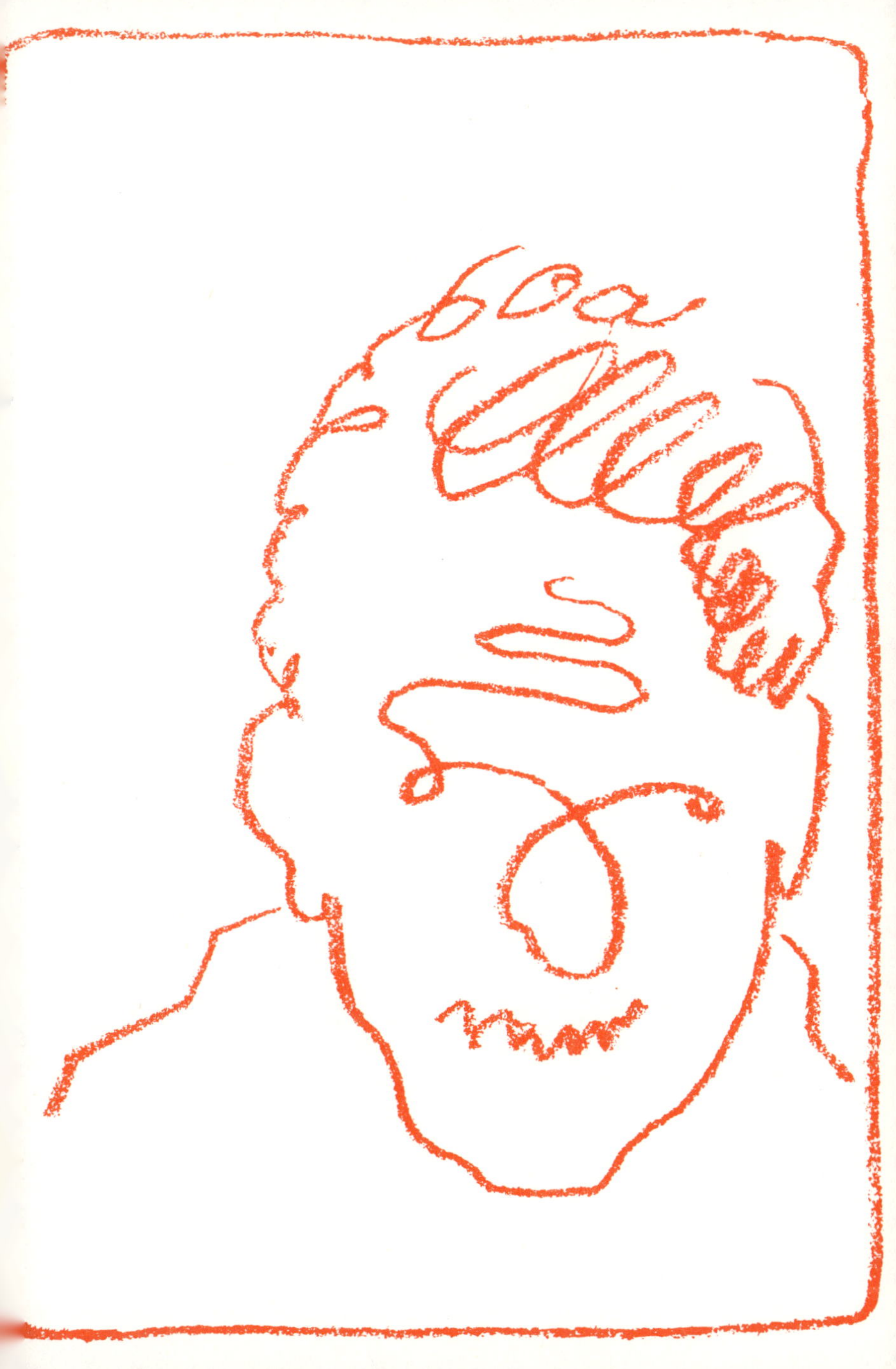

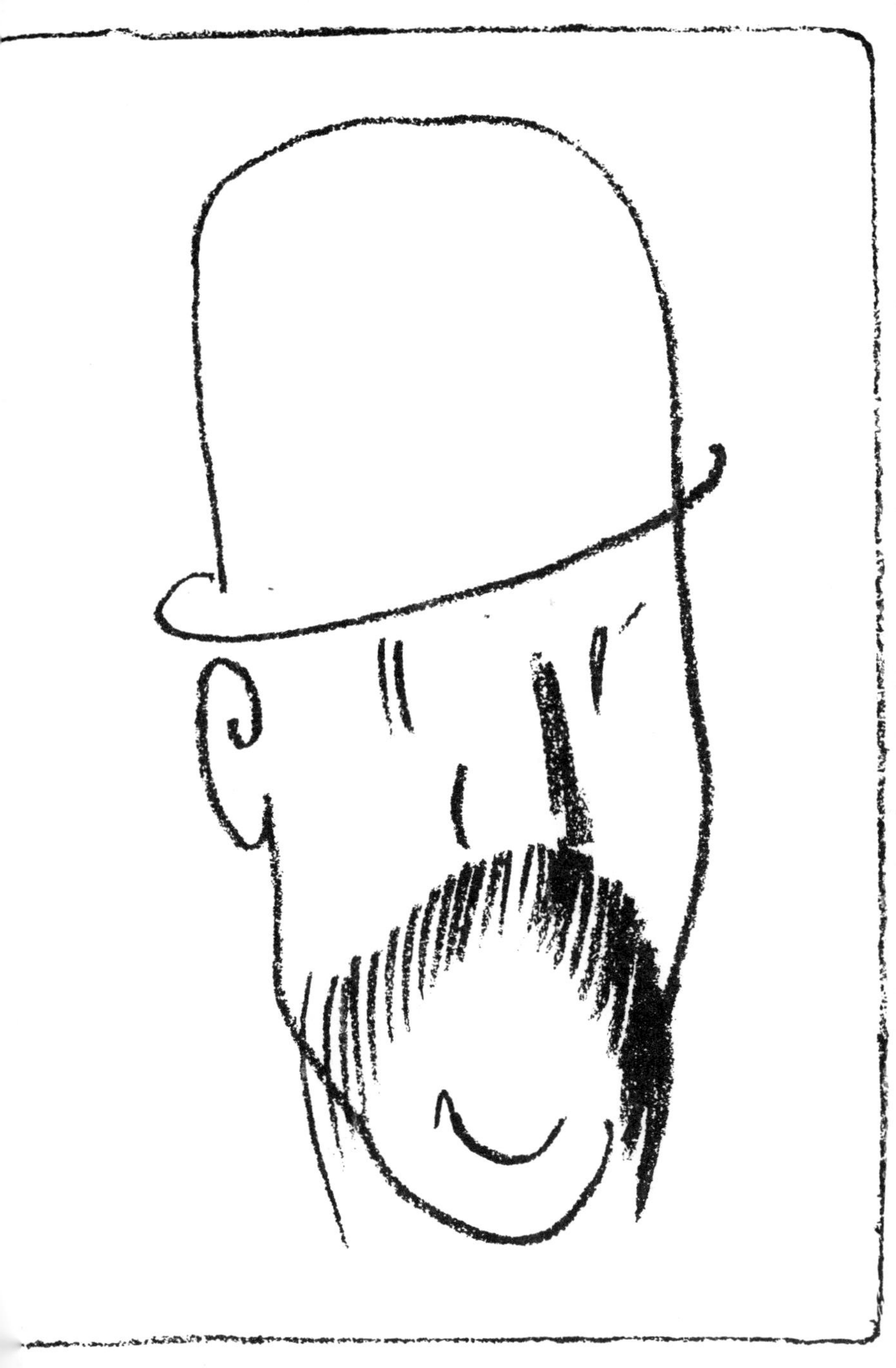

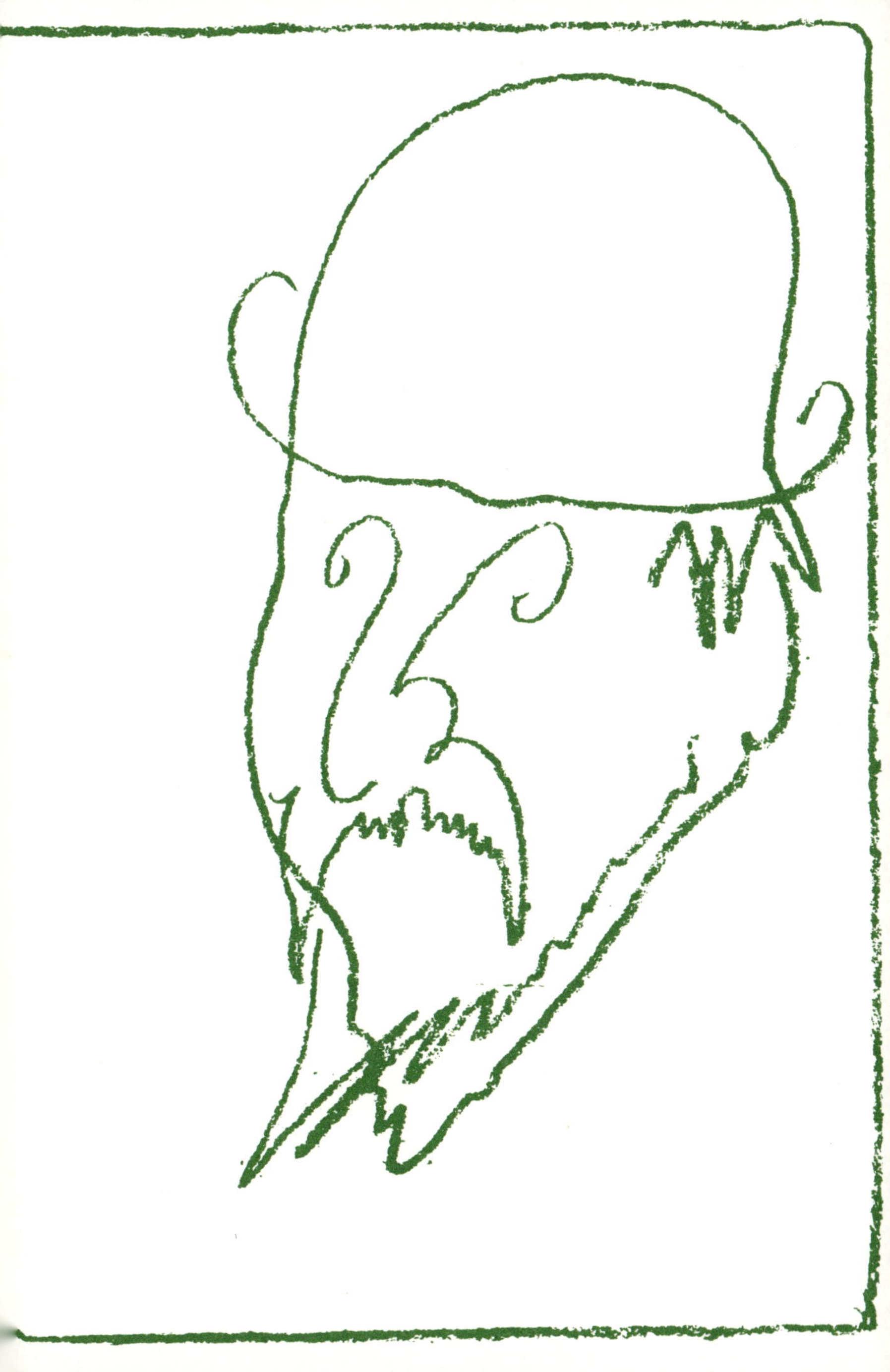

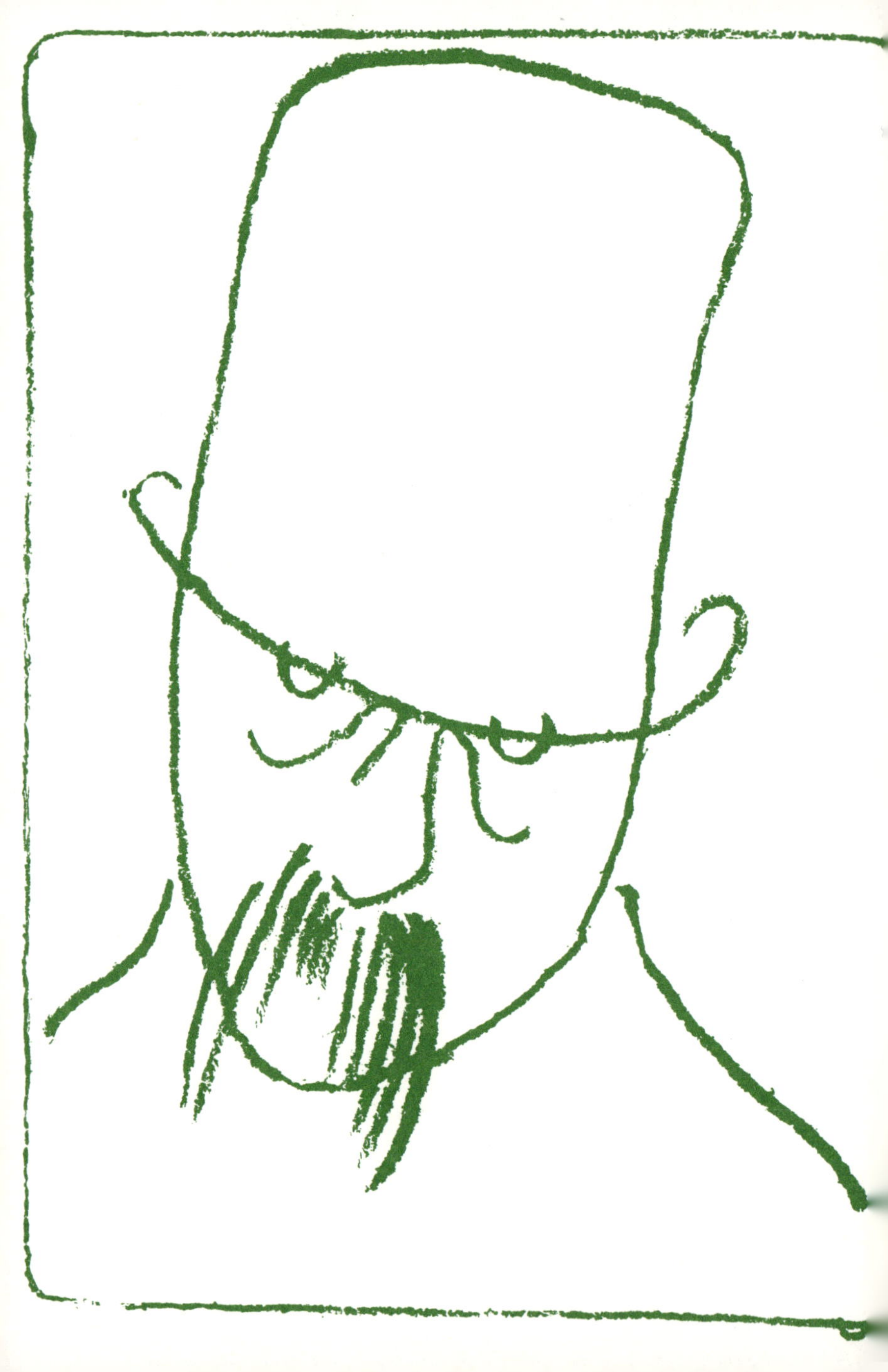

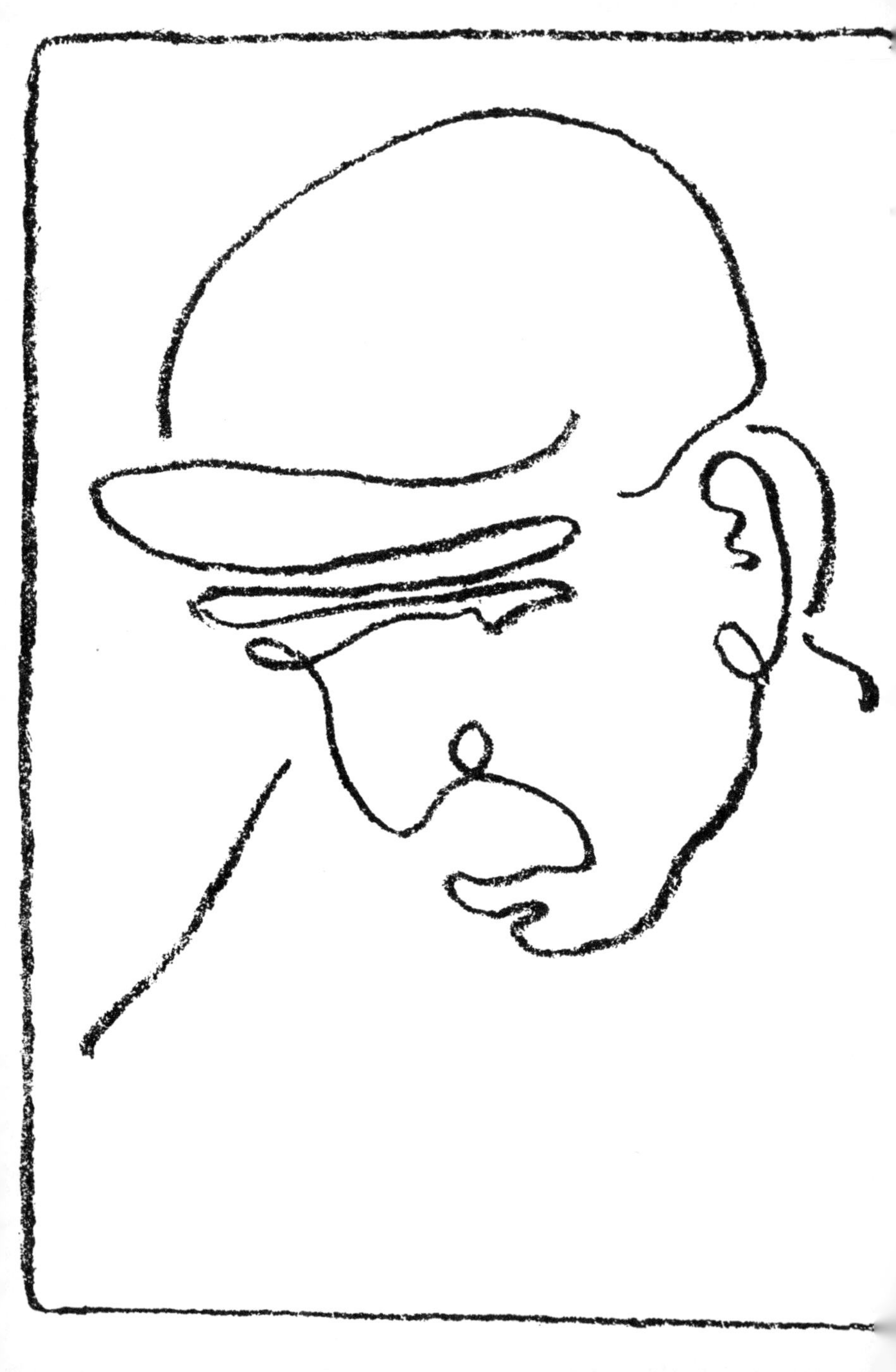

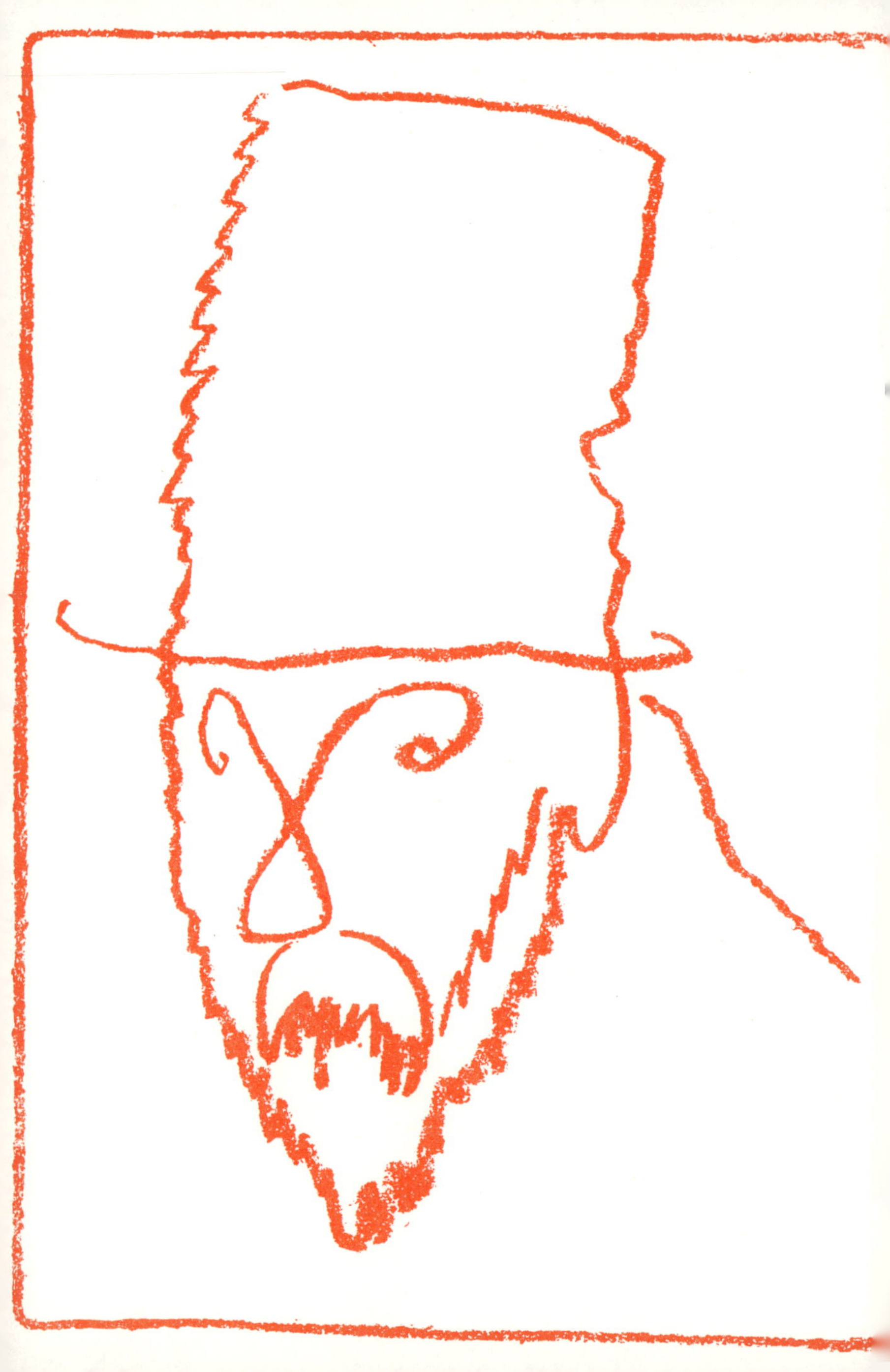

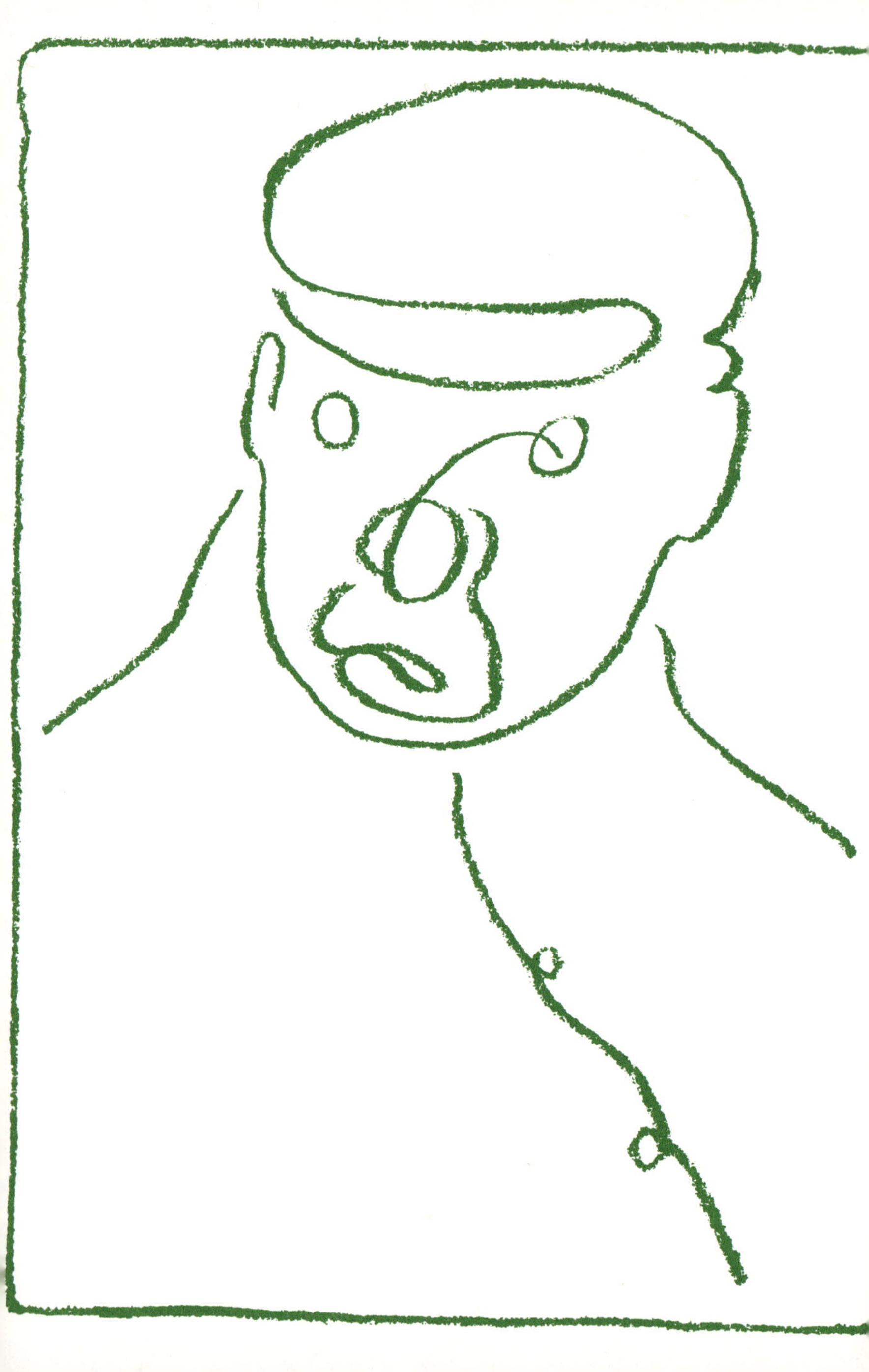

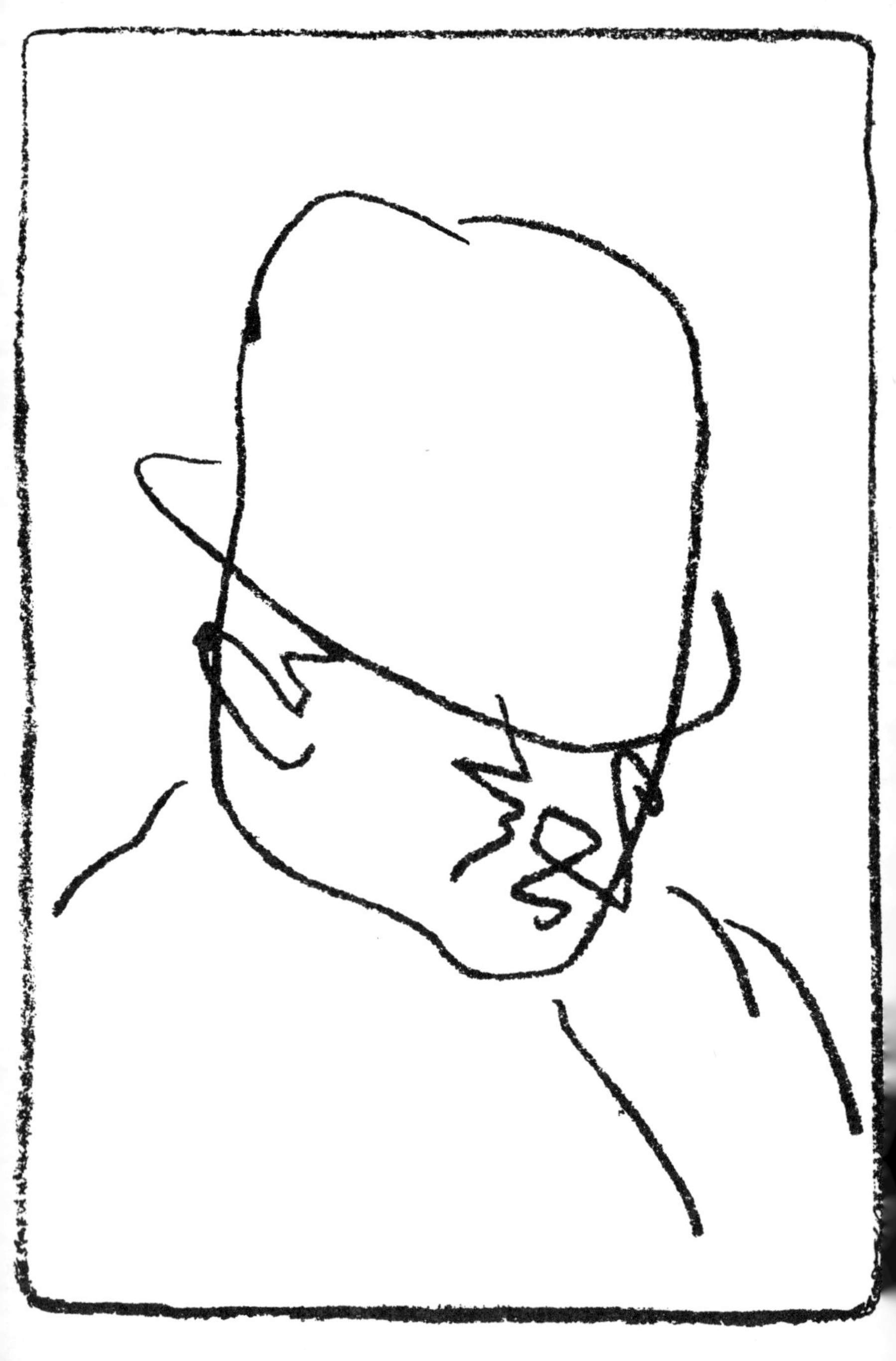

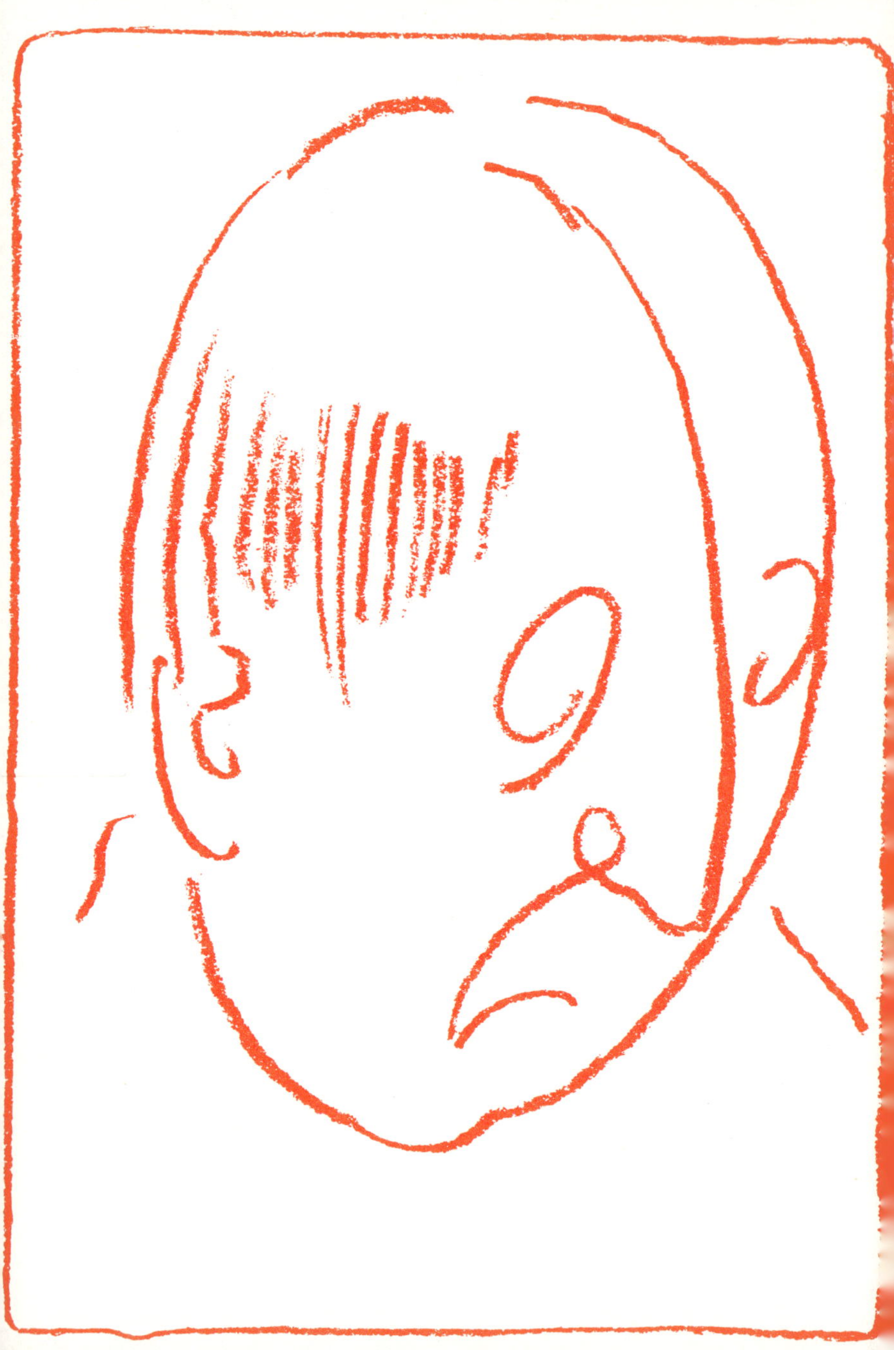

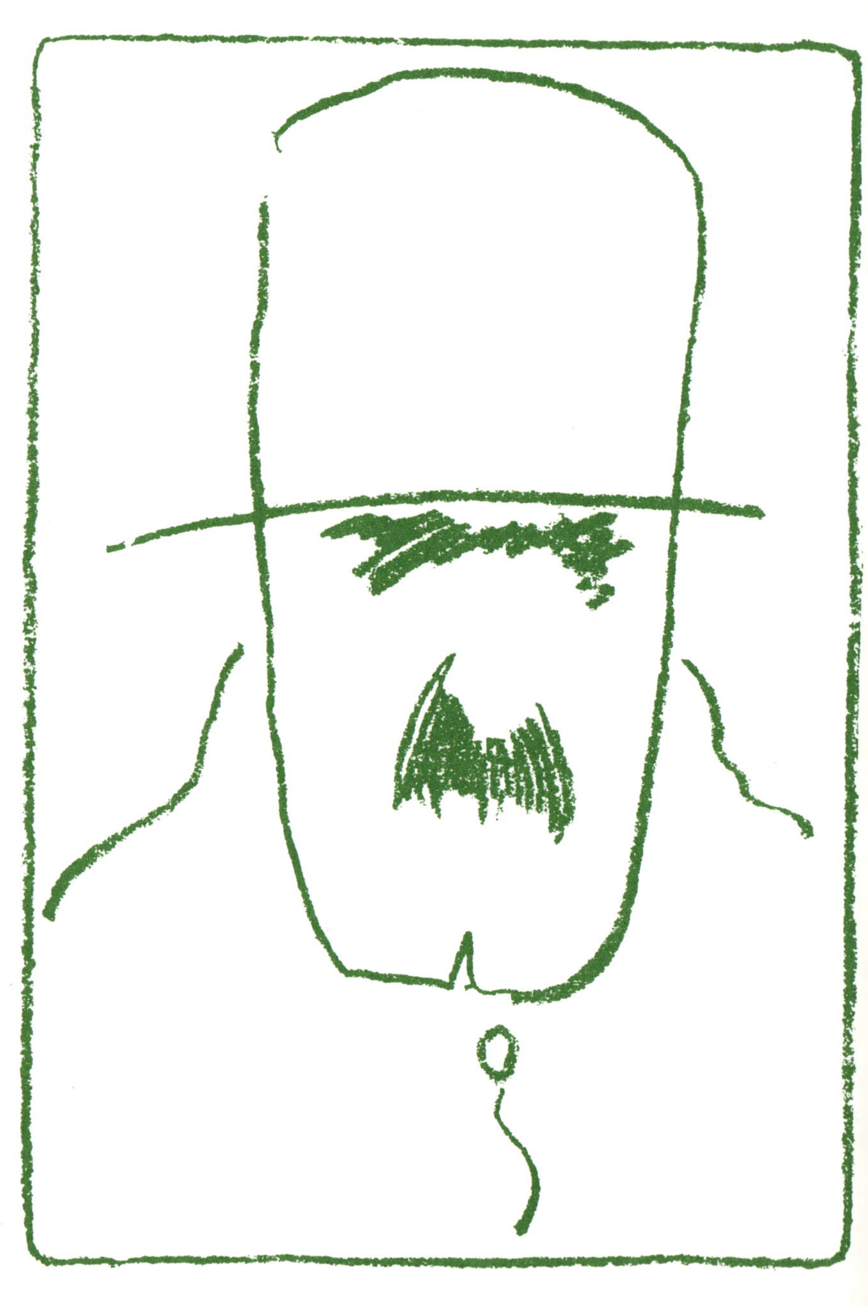

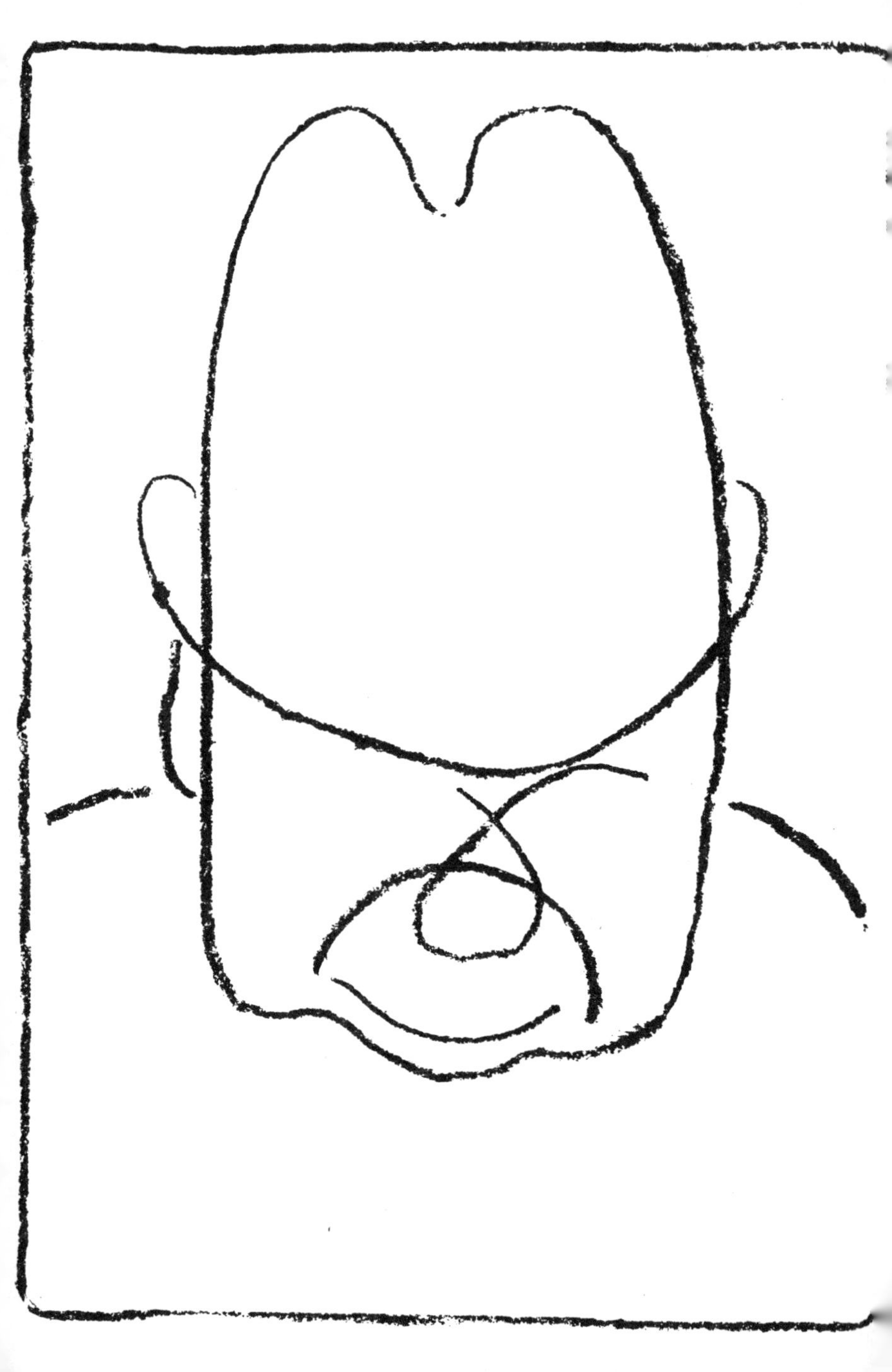

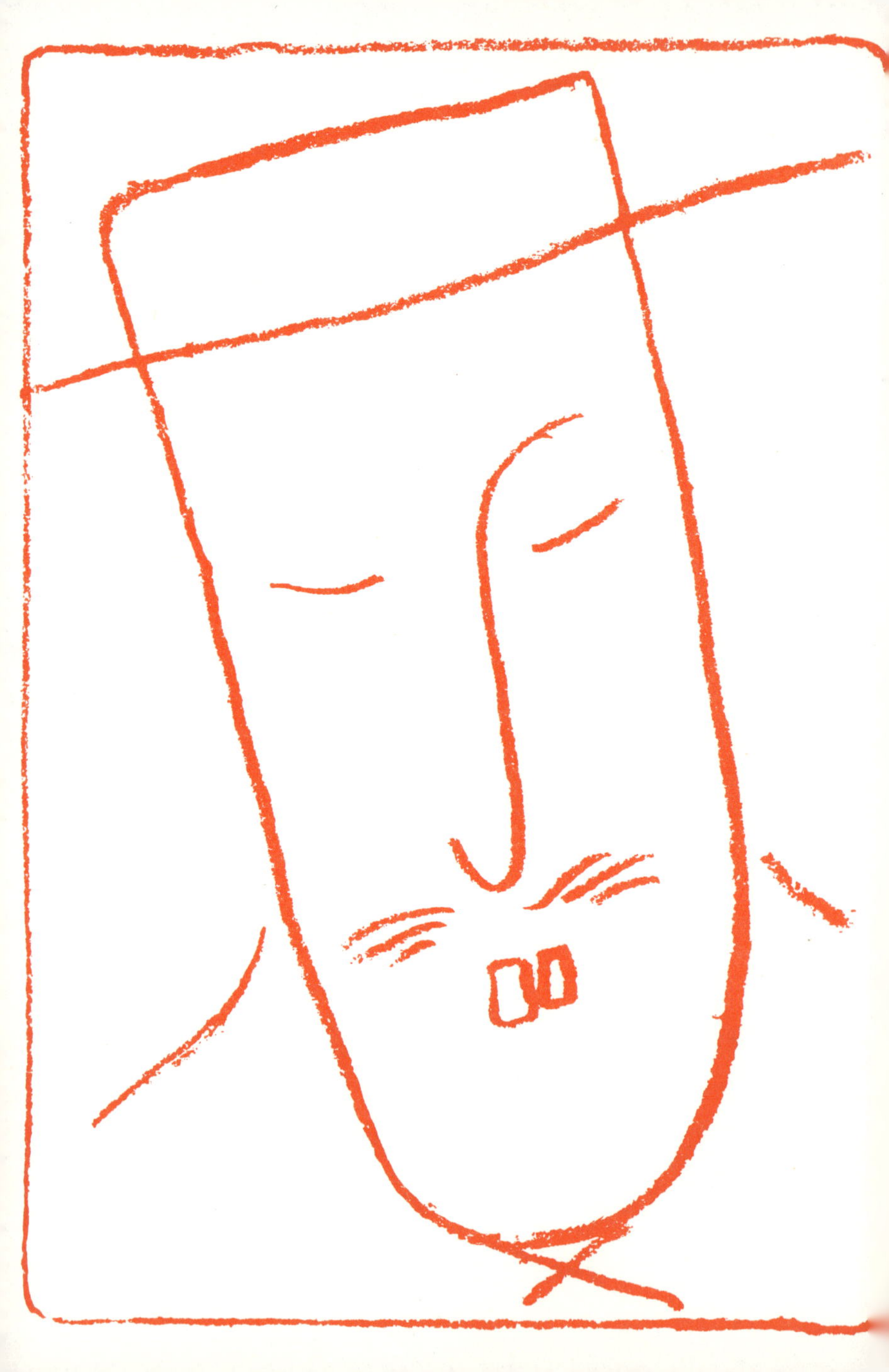

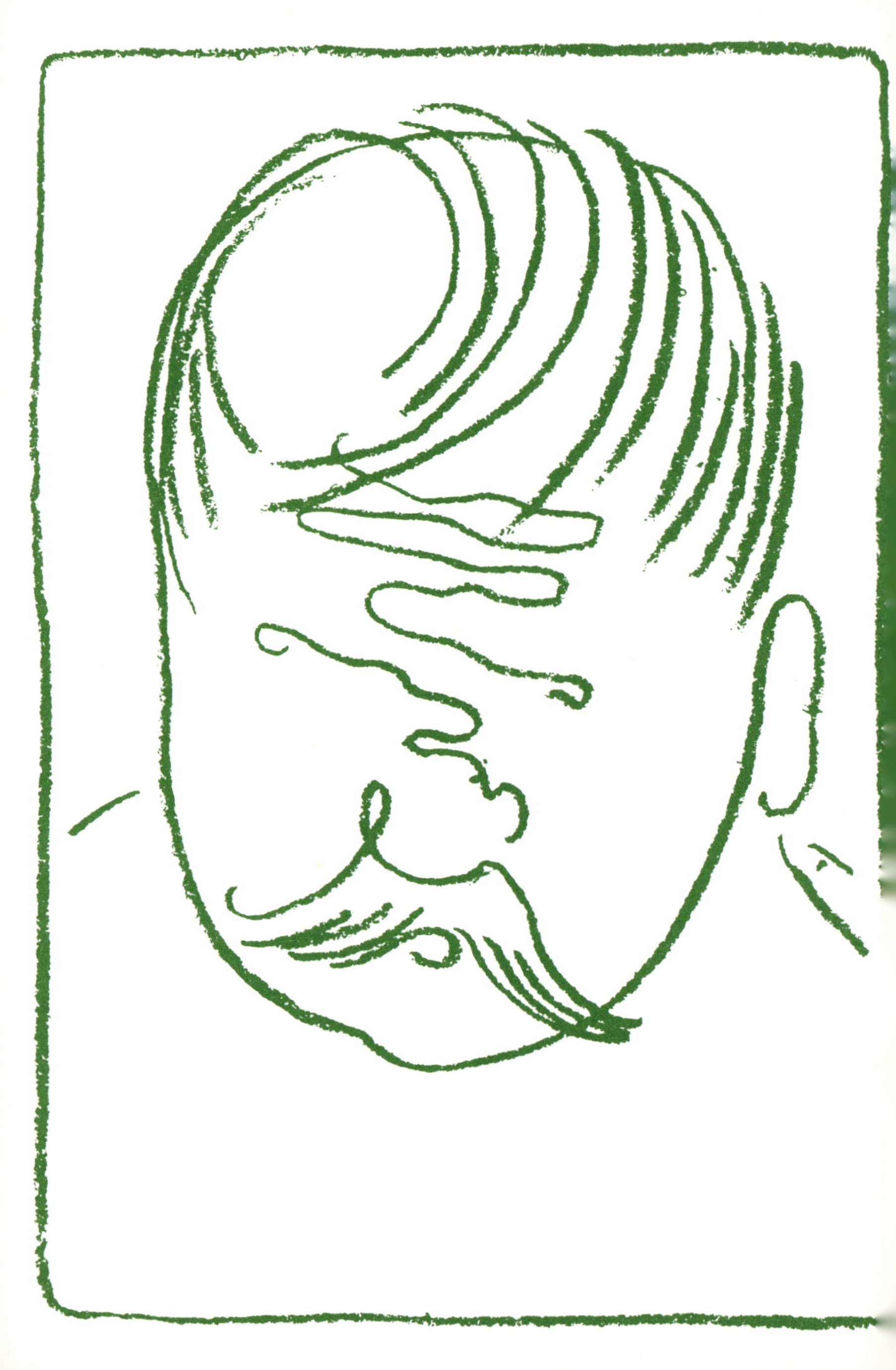

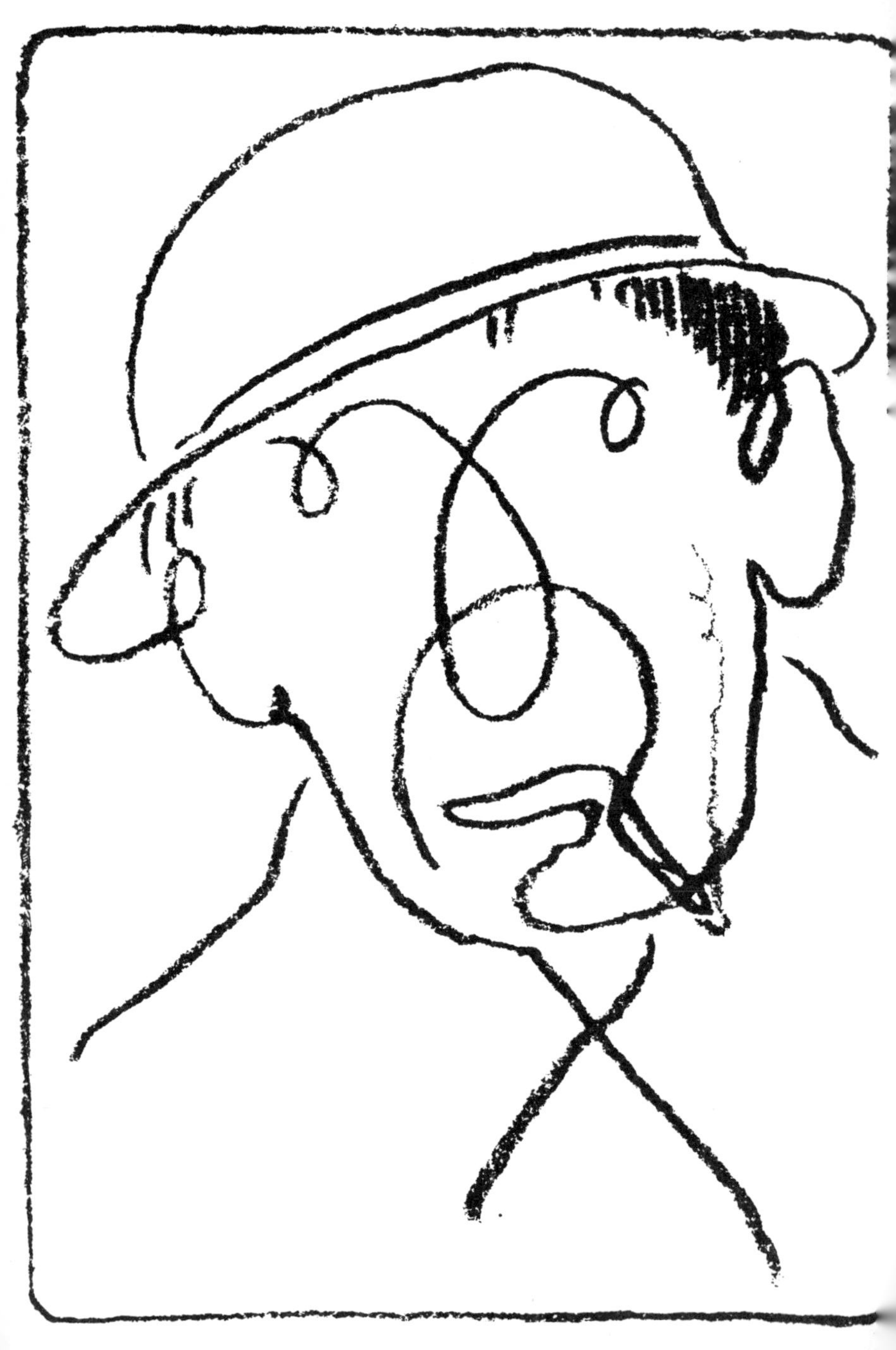

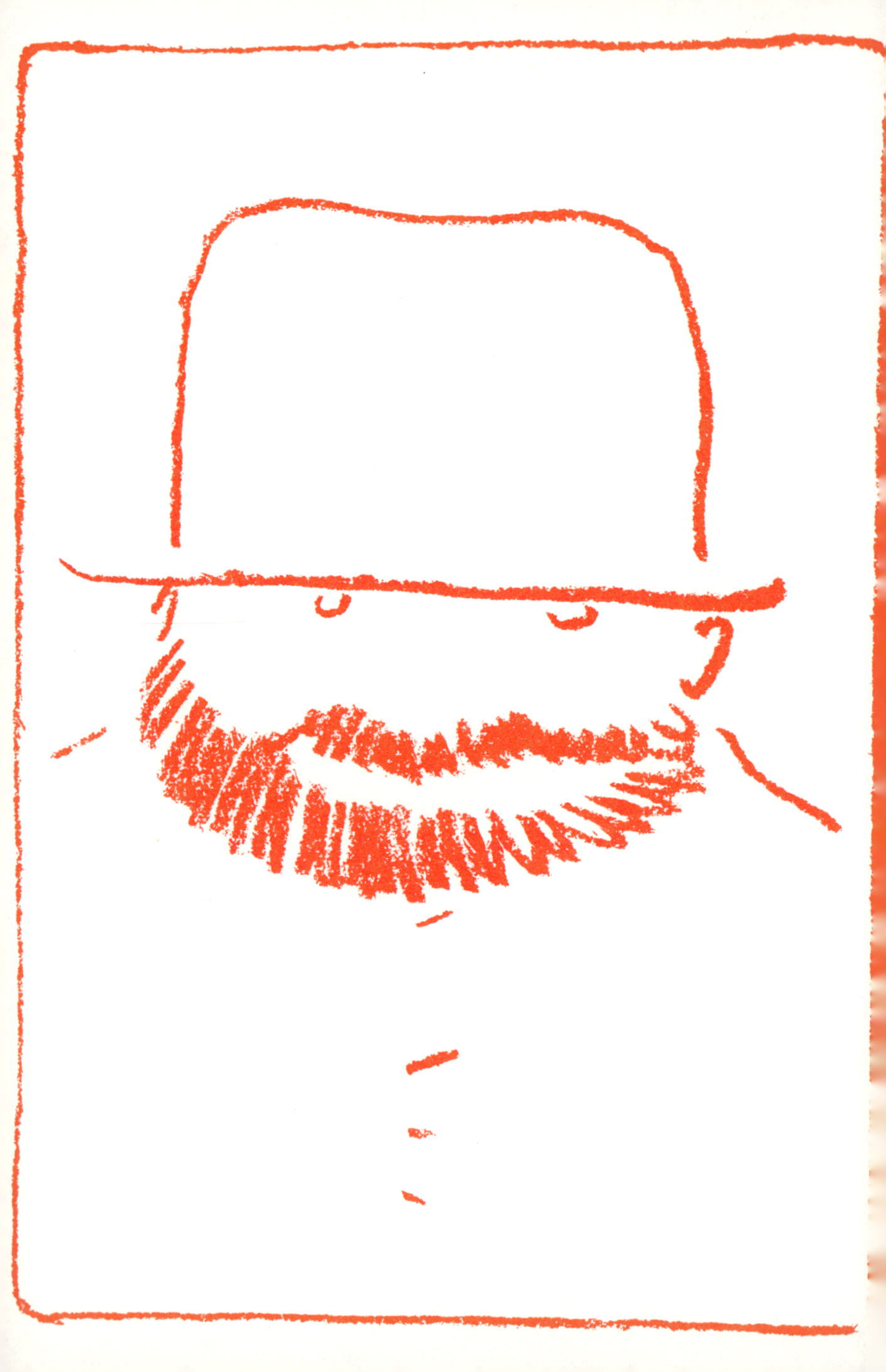

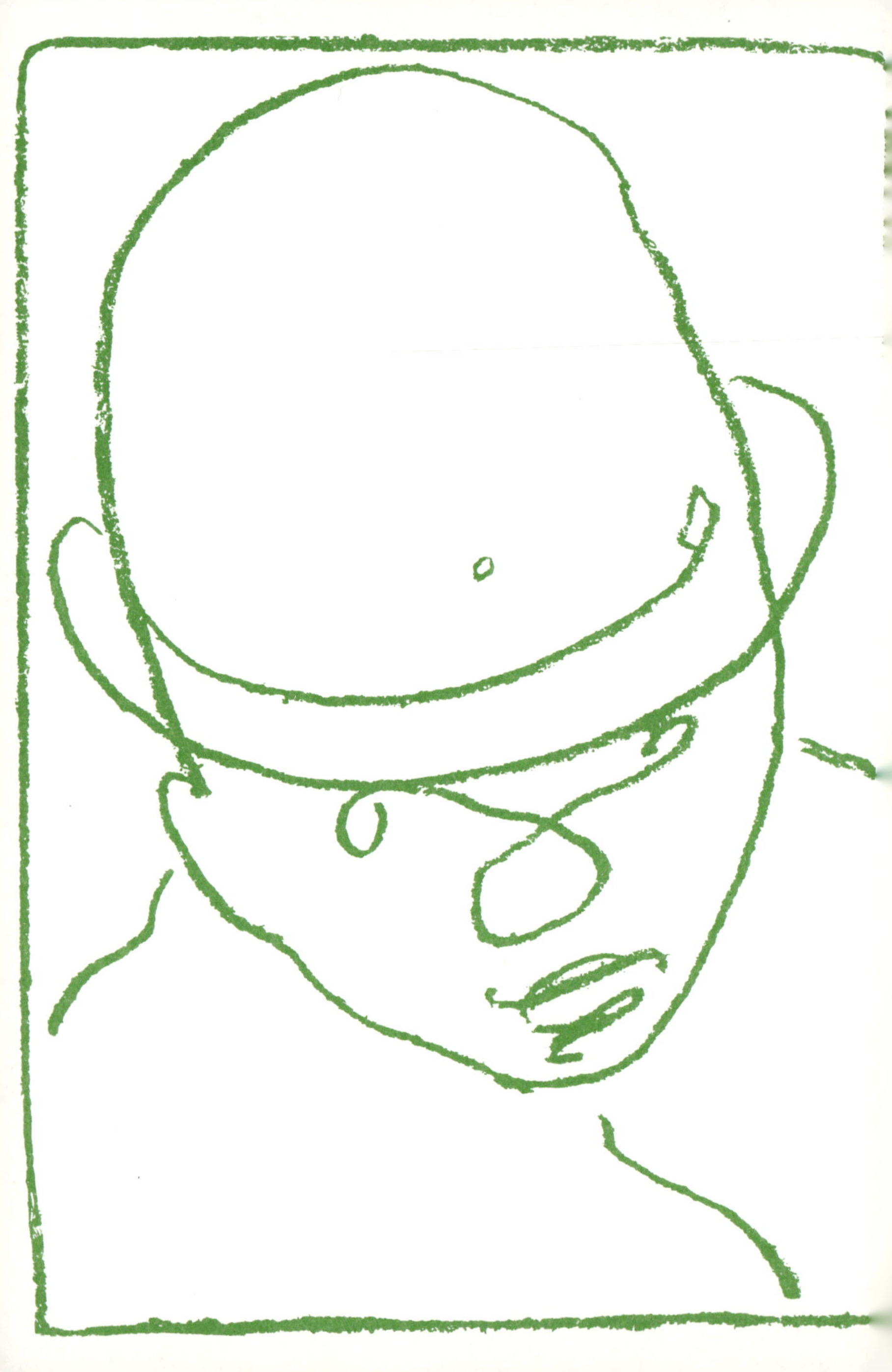

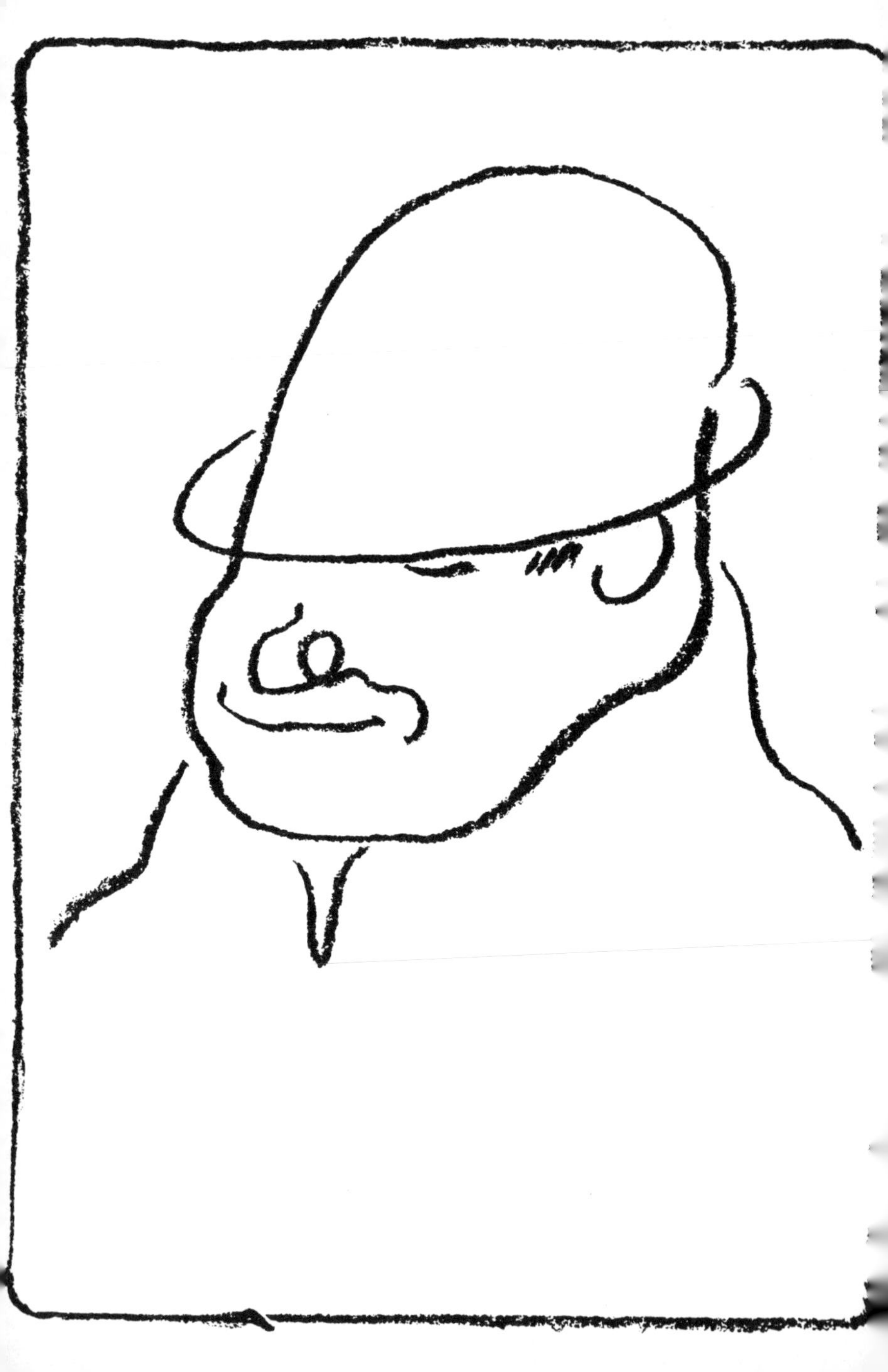

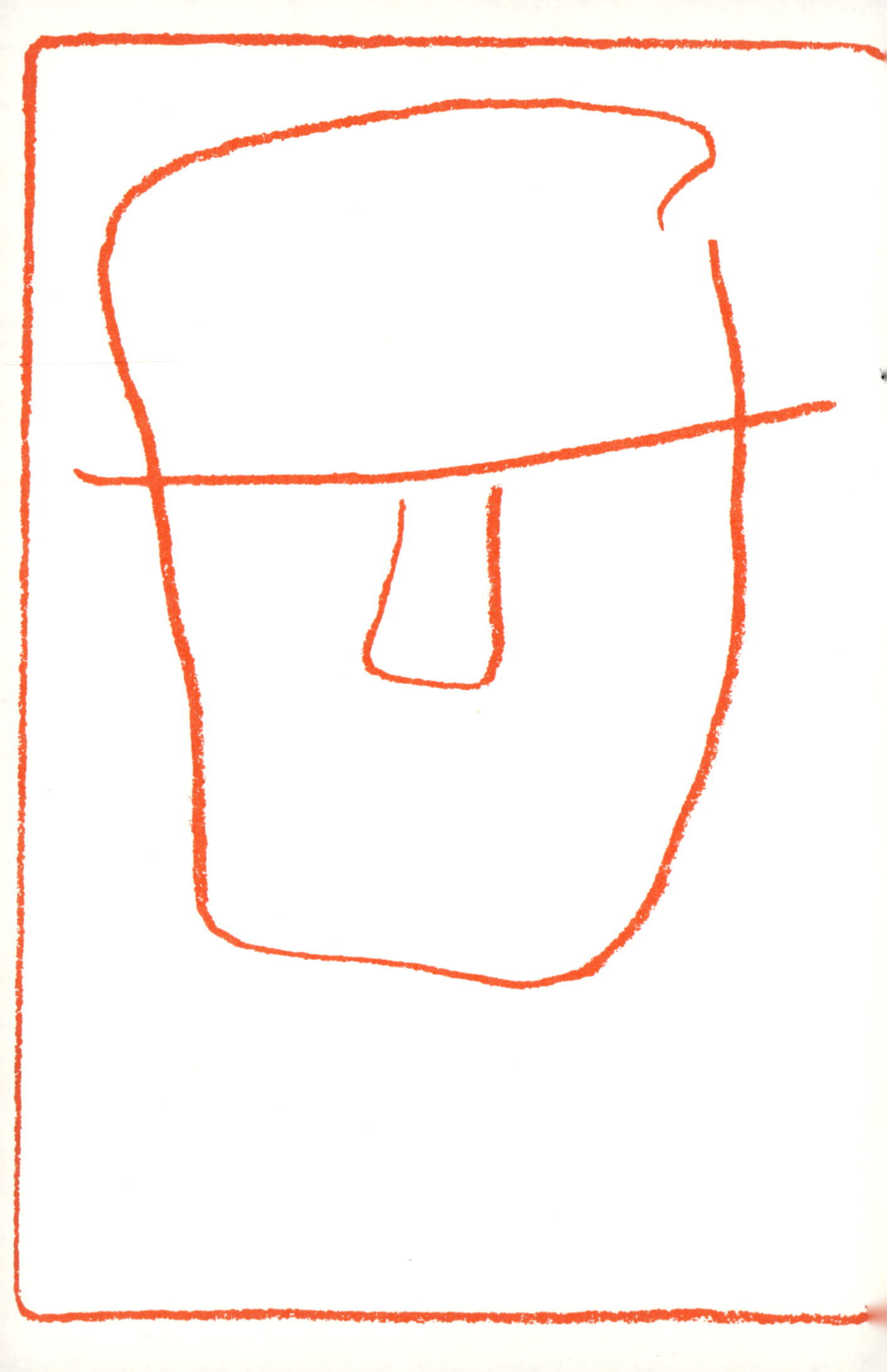

THE BOOK OF BLOKES
by William Nicholson
First published 1929
This edition first published 2026
by Pallas Athene (Publishers) Ltd
2 Birch Close, London N19 5XD
www.pallasathene.co.uk
ISBN 978 1 84368 278 3
Printed in China

William Nicholson (1872–1949), 'so fertile in grotesque invention' in the words of Max Beerbohm, began drawing 'bloke' faces for his daughter and for friends in the mid-1920s. The aim was to use as few lines as possible and to try not to lift the pencil from the paper. In 1929 Nicholson made a set for publication as a Christmas book; he hoped that Beerbohm, its dedicatee, would write an introduction but this never materialised. The book became a firm favourite of the artist's: 'I think our "Blokes" do us credit, don't you?' he wrote to the publisher, 'their colour is charming and I trust they will give a good imitation of the hottest cakes.' He himself gave many copies away for Christmas and birthdays.